U.S. HISTORY IN REVIEW

The Transcontinental Railroad

Emmett Martin

Enslow PUBLISHING

Please visit our website, www.enslow.com. For a free color catalog of all our high-quality books, call toll free 1-800-398-2504 or fax 1-877-980-4454

Portions of this work were originally authored by John O'Mara and published as *The Transcontinental Railroad.* All new material this edition authored by Emmett Martin.

Cataloging-in-Publication Data
Names: Martin, Emmett.
Title: The Transcontinental Railroad / Emmett Martin.
Description: Buffalo, NY : Enslow Publishing, 2027. | Series: U.S. History in review | Includes glossary.
Identifiers: ISBN 9781978547193 (pbk.) | ISBN 9781978547209 (library bound) | ISBN 9781978547216 (ebook)
Subjects: LCSH: Railroads–United States–History–Juvenile literature.
Classification: LCC HE2751.M327 2027 | DDC 385.0978–dc23

Published in 2027 by
Enslow Publishing
2544 Clinton Street
Buffalo, NY 14224

Designer: Leslie Taylor
Interior layout: Tanya Dellaccio Keeney
Editor: Therese Shea

Photo credits: Series art (grunge flag) Andrey Kuzmin/Shutterstock.com; series art (stamp icon) Stocker_team/Shutterstock.com; series art (font) santstock/Shutterstock.com; series art (swash) BUTENKOV ALEKSEI/Shutterstock.com; cover, p. 27 https://upload.wikimedia.org/wikipedia/commons/5/5d/East_and_West_Shaking_hands_at_the_laying_of_last_rail_Union_Pacific_Railroad_-_Restoration.jpg; p. 5 Karel Bock/Shutterstock.com; p. 7 (top) https://upload.wikimedia.org/wikipedia/commons/d/d7/Steam_Engine_-_an_ad_in_Matchetts_Baltimore_Director_1831.jpg; p. 7 (bottom) Historic Collection/Alamy Images; p. 9 (top) https://upload.wikimedia.org/wikipedia/commons/6/65/44._Cape_Horn%2C_C.P.R.R.jpg; p. 9 (bottom) https://upload.wikimedia.org/wikipedia/commons/1/1e/CPRR_Chief_Engineer_Theodore_D._Judah.jpg; p. 11 https://upload.wikimedia.org/wikipedia/commons/f/fe/Abraham_Lincoln_seated%2C_Feb_9%2C_1864.jpg; p. 13 yhelfman/Shutterstock.com; p. 15 (top) https://upload.wikimedia.org/wikipedia/commons/e/e8/San_Francisco_Pacific_Railroad_Bond_WPRR_1865.jpg; p. 15 (bottom) https://upload.wikimedia.org/wikipedia/commons/6/61/Trestle_CPRR.jpg; p. 17 CBW/Alamy Images; p. 19 North Wind Picture Archives/Alamy Images; p. 21 (top) https://upload.wikimedia.org/wikipedia/commons/c/cf/Dale_Creek_Bridge_Union_Pacific_Railroad_Company_by_Andrew_J_Russell.jpg; p. 21 (bottom) Courtesy of the Library of Congress; p. 23 https://upload.wikimedia.org/wikipedia/commons/c/cc/Golden_Spike_National_Historic_Site_GOSP4964.jpg; p. 25 (top) Vlad Ra27/Shutterstock.com; p. 25 https://upload.wikimedia.org/wikipedia/commons/8/83/Reno_to_Virginia_City_NV_CPRR-V%26TRR_Ticket_1878_.jpg; p. 29 https://upload.wikimedia.org/wikipedia/commons/e/e9/TranscontinentalPoster.jpg.

Printed in the United States of America

CPSIA compliance information: Batch #CSENS27: For further information, contact Enslow Publishing, New York, New York, at 1-800-398-2504.

Contents

*Words in the glossary appear in **bold** the first time they are used in the text.*

Difficult Journeys

In the early United States, Americans couldn't travel far easily or quickly. People traveled on foot or by horseback. Some traveled in slow-moving wagons or **stagecoaches**. The trip from coast to coast was *really* hard. Even the journeys by ship were long, hard, and costly. Railroads changed travel forever.

Learn More

Those traveling by ship from coast to coast could sail around South America. Others sailed to Central America, traveled to the other side, and sailed up the coast.

Early Railroads

Construction for the first U.S. railroad started in 1828. Railroads made travel between large cities easier. Soon came the idea for a transcontinental railroad, or train tracks that crossed the whole country. It would be a hard job.

Learn More

The first U.S. steam **locomotive** was called *Tom Thumb*. Before this, trains were drawn by horses.

Theodore Judah

Engineer Theodore Judah explored many **routes** for a transcontinental railroad. In 1860, he found a good path through the Sierra Nevada mountains. He found **investors** for the railroad, and he gained support from the U.S. government. Judah died in 1863 before the railroad was done.

Learn More

The first transcontinental railroad investors formed the Central Pacific Railroad Company, which would lay the tracks from California to the east.

Theodore Judah

Government Action

In July 1862, President Abraham Lincoln signed the Pacific Railway Act. This law provided land and money for the building of a railroad across the nation. It also created the Union Pacific Railroad, which would lay the tracks from east to west.

Learn More

The Pacific Railway Act was signed during the American Civil War. This was the war fought from 1861 to 1865 between the Northern states and the Southern states.

Abraham Lincoln

Both the Union Pacific Railroad and Central Pacific Railroad companies were given government bonds to help pay for the great cost of construction. Bonds are a kind of loan that has to be paid back with more money, called interest. The more tracks laid, the more bonds the companies received.

Learn More

The companies received larger bonds through more difficult terrain, or land, such as mountains.

Getting Started

Central Pacific Railroad workers began construction of a track in Sacramento, California, in 1863 and moved east. Union Pacific workers began laying tracks after the American Civil War ended in 1865. They built from Omaha, Nebraska, and moved west.

railroad bond

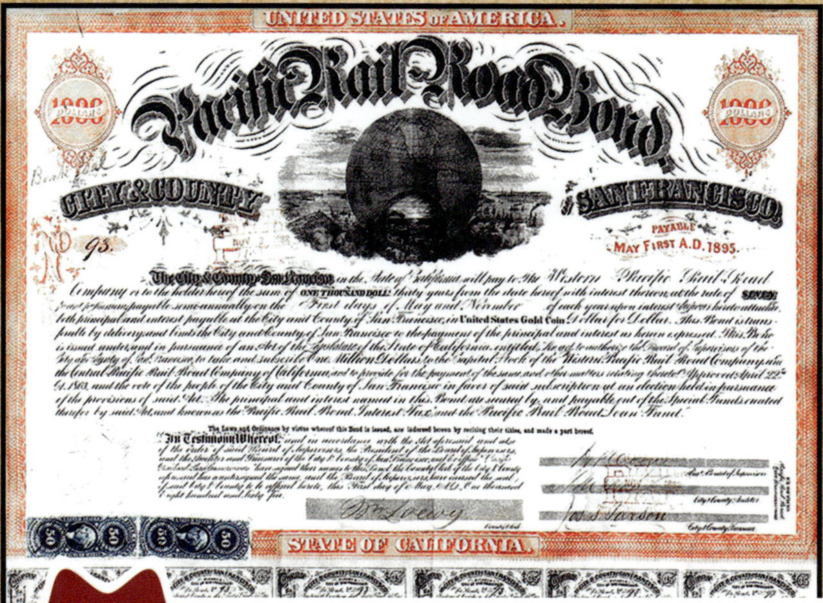

Learn More

In 1864, the second Pacific Railway Act gave more land to the railroads. The railroads sold bonds and land to raise more money for building.

Who Did the Work?

Construction of the railroad required many workers. The Union Pacific hired many Irish **immigrants** as well as men who had been Civil War soldiers. They also hired **Mormons** to lay tracks through Utah, where many had settled. Work went fast across flat terrain.

Learn More

The railroad companies laid tracks across the lands of Native Americans including the Lakota Sioux and Pawnee. Railroads affected hunting and other ways of life. Some Native Americans attacked workers or the tracks themselves.

General John S. Casement of the Union Pacific Railroad

The Central Pacific Railroad struggled to find enough **laborers** to do the difficult work. The company began hiring Chinese immigrants. By 1867, Chinese laborers made up about 90 percent of the Central Pacific's workforce, or about 14,000 people.

Learn More

Chinese railroad workers were often treated unfairly, including making less money than white workers.

Great Dangers

Railroad work was dangerous. Central Pacific workers had to blast through mountains with **explosives**. They built high wooden bridges over valleys. Workers died of the cold and in **avalanches** too. Hundreds of laborers died in the Sierra Nevada.

Learn More

In 1867, Chinese workers went on **strike** and asked for higher pay. The Central Pacific Railroad wouldn't send food until they ended the strike.

Race to the End

By early 1869, the Central Pacific and Union Pacific tracks were close. The companies agreed to meet at Promontory Summit in Utah. Workers raced to finish their tracks. In April, Central Pacific laid 10 miles (16 km) of track in one day, breaking the Union Pacific's record of 8.5 miles (14 km).

Learn More

The two railroad companies were in such a hurry that they built past each other at first!

The Final Numbers

In all, Union Pacific laid about 1,086 miles (1,748 km). Central Pacific laid about 690 miles (1,110 km) of track. Central Pacific had begun laying tracks earlier than Union Pacific. However, they completed fewer miles because of the mountainous terrain.

Learn More

Some worker camps along the routes became towns and cities. Cheyenne, Wyoming, began this way in 1867.

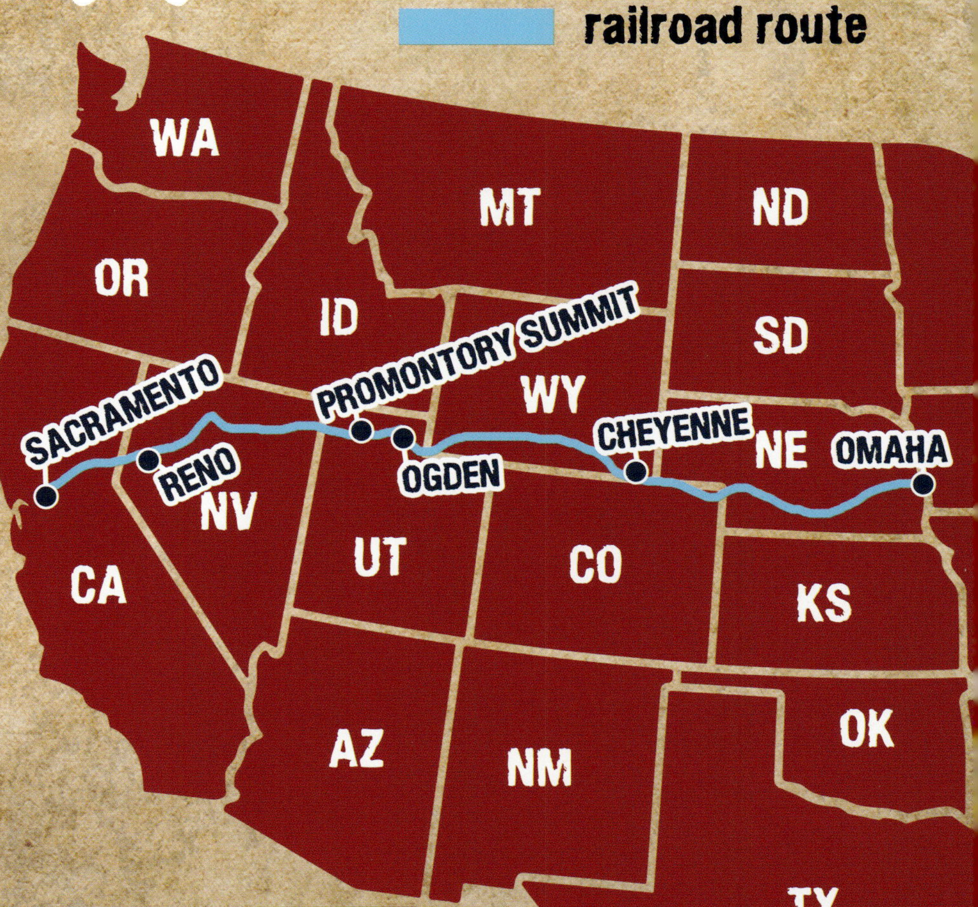

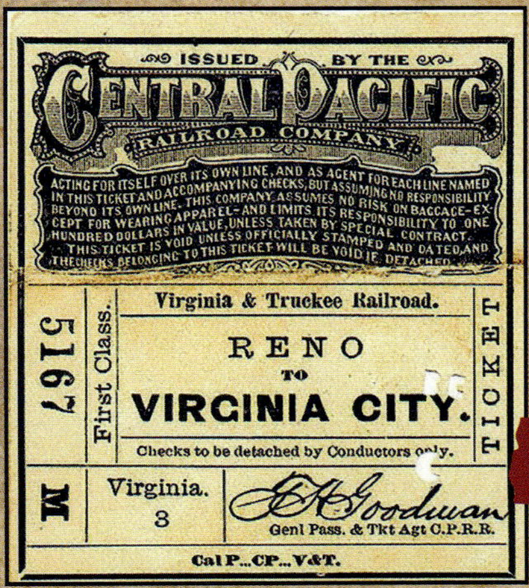

railroad ticket

Uniting the Tracks

A special event was held at Promontory Summit on May 10, 1869, to officially join the tracks. Central Pacific president Leland Stanford and Union Pacific vice president Thomas Durant tapped gold and silver spikes into the tracks. These were then replaced with iron spikes.

Learn More

When the last spike went in, a **telegraph** message was sent out that read: D-O-N-E.

Changing Times

The Central Pacific and Union Pacific tracks connected to other existing railroads. By rail, someone could cross the nation in less than 2 weeks, cutting the trip by many months. Goods could be shipped more places too. The transcontinental railroad changed the nation.

Learn More

The transcontinental railroad brought people across and to Native American lands. Many Native Americans were forced to move.

A Timeline of the Transcontinental Railroad

1860
Engineer Theodore Judah finds the best route for a transcontinental railroad through the Sierra Nevada.

1861
The American Civil War begins.

1862
President Abraham Lincoln signs the Pacific Railway Act to support the building of the railroad.

1863
The Central Pacific Railroad starts laying track east from Sacramento, California.

1864
Lincoln signs another act that gives more land and larger bonds to the railroad companies.

1865
The American Civil War ends. The Union Pacific begins laying track west.

1869
On April 28, Central Pacific workers lay a record amount of tracks in a single day.

On May 10, the Central Pacific and Union Pacific rail lines join at Promontory Summit, Utah.

Glossary

avalanche: A large mass of snow, rocks, or ice sliding down a mountain or over a cliff.

construction: Having to do with the act of building something.

engineer: Someone who plans or oversees the building of something.

explosive: A kind of matter or device that produces a powerful blast.

immigrant: One who comes to a country to settle there.

investor: One who spends money to make more money in the future.

laborer: One who works.

locomotive: The wheeled machine that produces the power to pull a train.

Mormon: A member of a Christian church founded in the United States in 1830.

route: A course that people travel.

stagecoach: A closed, horse-drawn wagon used to carry people and mail.

strike: A stopping of work by employees as a protest against an employer.

telegraph: A method of communicating using electric signals sent through wires.

For More Information

Books

Hirsch, Andy. *The Transcontinental Railroad: Crossing the Divide*. New York, NY: First Second, 2022.

Nnachi, Ngeri. *The Real History of the Transcontinental Railroad*. Minneapolis, MN: Lerner Publications, 2023.

Website

Transcontinental Railroad
kids.britannica.com/students/article/transcontinental-railroad/629320
Read more about the history behind this railroad.

Publisher's note to educators and parents: *Our editors have carefully reviewed these websites to ensure that they are suitable for students. Many websites change frequently, however, and we cannot guarantee that a site's future contents will continue to meet our high standards of quality and educational value. Be advised that students should be closely supervised whenever they access the internet.*

Index